Wonderland

A Collection of Poems
by Breanna Tupac

Copyright © **by Breanna Tupac** All Rights Reserved
No part of this book may be reproduced or used in any manner without written permission of the copyright owner except for quotation in a book review.

First Edition December 2020

By the Sea

At the peak of the cliff,
Hanging above the sea.
There is a place that we would visit
Every year to see.
Lights everywhere, all around.
Lights on top of a garden,
With not a single rose to be found.
It didn't matter that we saw the same lights
Every year.
Just being with you,
Brought me so much cheer.
We filled with amazement,
At the same beautiful display,
As if it were the first time
Not every year on this day.

We would stay very shortly,
It was too cold to stay.
But we enjoyed every second
Before we went home that day.

The love of my life,
With lights sparkling in your eyes.
Made my whole world turn upside down.
My feet in the skies.

Being with you every day is a treasure.
Though the light in your eyes,
Better than beyond measure.

I loved you then,
And I love you still.
I love you today,
And I always will.

Today by the Christmas tree,
I can see those lights in your eyes once again.
And after this Christmas,
I will wait until next year,
Happily until then.

Sound of Home

I don't remember too much about my childhood.
Only a thing here or there, or two.
But I remember the smell in the wintertime,
As a teenager, I do.
I remember being by the tree,
Laying with a festive blanket, warm and cozy.
My parent's dog in my lap, such a good boy.
He would lean up and give me kisses,
I am still grateful for that.
I remember the sound of my siblings laughing,
Somewhere in the back.
Then I remember it falling quiet.
Not even a mouse,
Was heard.
It felt ever so peaceful, yet the quiet almost hurt.
As I yearned for the noises I had heard once before.

Now as an adult, who has since moved away.
I wish I could time travel, back to that day.
Just for a minute, or maybe two.
To remember the times when I just laid on the couch With my parent's dog.
Listening to my siblings laughter,
In the light of the tree.

Christmas in Quarantine

This time of year,
Usually fills me with cheer.
Though it's hard to be cheery,
When the world around me looks so dreary.

I wanted to enjoy this time,
But it feels more alone.
All I really wanted,
Was to be able to go home.
To spend Christmas with family,
To see their faces that day.
Though to keep them safe,
We must stay away.

I want to be strong,
Really, I do.
It's just hard to get through the holidays,
Without all of you.

I miss my dad's hugs, my mother's too.
I miss my siblings fighting.
Weirdly, it's true.

I miss the pumpkin roll,
And I missed spending Thanksgiving with you.

I know Christmas will be more of the same,
A certain something missing.
A friend, a family name.

I just hope that next year,
We can be together,
Bringing one another cheer.

February Baby

I look at you, sound asleep.
Wondering what you are dreaming of,
If you're dreaming of me.
Almost two years old at this point,
With a birthday coming up fast.
I had no idea really just how short the baby years
Were actually going to last.

Born in the winter, but thrived in the summertime.
My little February baby,
You are growing and learning just fine.
Though mom is not ready,
Maybe I never will be.
I am not ready to see you grow into the man
I know you are going to be.

But the time is getting closer, whether I like it or not.
With each passing year,
My heart becomes a tighter knot.

You are my sunshine, and I love you so.
You are my forever my baby,
Even after you grow.

Vacation Elves

I always wondered what Santa's elves did
The rest of the year.
Do they still work to bring the children cheer?
Do they get sick of the holiday?
Sick of their jobs?
Or do they love every second of it all?

Do they go on vacation?
If they did, where would they go?
I imagine an elf in swim trunks
Lounging by a pool in the Caribbean.
A yellow towel by their side.

Or would they go to Paris,
And sip coffee, while reading a book.
Go to Africa on safari,
Just to get a good look
At all the wildlife.

Would they travel to Australia,
To surf and swim with dolphins?
Would they go to India, to the Taj Mahal?
Visit every Wonder of the World?

Would they come to America,
To each coast? Everything in between?
I wonder which one they would prefer the most.

What if they had hobbies, other than work.
Just imagine an elf, on the search for Bigfoot!
Or maybe one likes to paint,
Or even play video games!
One that likes to cook, and one likes to make music.

They might all look the same, but if they were one on one, how different would they really be?
I wonder if they went of vacation,
If they would ever take me.

I would be in to go for a swim with a
Vacation Elf.
To travel to the Bahamas,
Both in search of ourselves.

So this year on my list,
I have been as specific as I can.

Dear Santa,
All I want for Christmas this year,
               Is a Vacation Elf.
                               With Love, Yours Truly.

Winter List

1. Snow on the ground
2. Lights strung around
3. Bells ringing
4. Carolers singing
5. Trees decorated
6. Each other's company celebrated
7. Stocking's hung
8. Poems sung
9. Children playing
10. Kittens laying
11. Nativity scene on display
12. Baby Jesus laying in a bed of hay
13. Wise men reading
14. Old dogs sleeping
15. Couple's kissing
16. Kettle's hissing
17. Turkey's been cooked
18. Ornaments hooked
19. Elves start to say
20. Santa Claus is on his way

Sleepwalking

As I lie my head to sleep tonight,
I whisper half a gleam.
I wish to dream of lighter things,
And forget about myself.
I wish to go to distance lands,
And swim with dolphins worry free.
I wish to fly away tonight,
To wander aimlessly.

I seek the guidance of a friend,
As all my dreams come caving in.
Though I dread not the morning light,
As my freedom goes bleak.
Freedom comes with a price,
But the price for mine is sleep.

For when I wake,
The little monster plays,
And I join him happily.

He wakes me up with a smile,
Making my freedom a worry of the past.
Each night I dream,
I know, and I pray,
That the feeling will soon pass.

Even though I am free as I dream,
My heart belongs to a little monster,
And his love sets me free.

Christmas Tree

The grown ups are sleeping now,
As I sneak through the hall.
I wander downstairs in search of something tall.
Entering the room with the couch, and armchair,
I see something brown,
With lots of green hair.

It's covered in small balls, and lights
That appear to be hung with some string.
I remember this green thing from last year I think.

I remember it making mommy smile,
And daddy too.
I wonder if they will smile at this one, I do.

But how did it get here? Where did it come from?
I wonder, but I am growing tiresome.
Time to go back to sleep, but I pray
That when I wake up, the green thing will have
stayed.

For when mommy and daddy see that it has come
today,
Their smiles will return,
And hopefully they'll stay.

Seasonal Sadness

That time of year has come around again.
When the days are much shorter,
And the sun shines less often.
Sometimes it feels like the sun
Takes all the happiness with it.

The rain begins to pour,
And plants begin to fade.
Trees lose their leaves,
As we all go about our days.

Some of us love this time of year,
Though some of us resent.
Some of us are comfortable,
The rest of us less than content.

Because with the rain comes darkness,
Outside, and in our minds.
Not everyone yearns for rainy days,
Or even cloudy times.

When the night comes,
That is the worst of all.
That's when the voices of others
Are nowhere to call.

Instead come the voices deep in our minds.
They yearn for the sunshine,
And let out bad thoughts in the dark.
They can be dangerous if they talk a lot.

We might love the weather, really we do.
Though with the dark days,
Our minds get darker too.

With seasons changing, we need to remember,
To check in with one another,
In the depth of December.

Seasonal Sadness comes for us all.
Just always remember,
That the sun always rises,
After it falls.

When the Snow Falls

When the snow falls,
I can hear his silent gasps.
My little one watches from the window,
Forgetting worries of his past.
His innocence makes me cheerful.
The light shining in his eyes,
So beautiful.

Then he looks over at me,
Smile spreading.
He comes, and cuddles with me,
As I had hoped this was where he was heading.

We sit next to the window,
Blanket around us.
Watching as if it were the very first snow,
And I'll cherish that moment for the both of us.

My Child

To me, a mother,
There is but one thing that I need.
That is you.

I don't need to have presents with my name
Under the Tree.
Those are all for you babe.
Hearing you say Mom,
That in itself is a dream come true.

I don't need jewelry,
Or a new scarf to prove your love.
You saying it is more than enough.

You are my rainbow,
My perfect baby boy.
That is the best gift I have ever received.
And I thank your dad every day,
For giving you to me.

So this year and every year to come,
Out of all the things you can get for me,
I only want some.

A hug, and a kiss.
And a day that goes by where I don't have to miss
Your beautiful face.

I want to see your smile as you look at the tree,
And hear you laugh as your dad tells a joke.

I want to hold you close,
Warm next to the fire.
If you want to know what I want,
That's all I desire.

There is nothing else I want from you,
Nothing to give.
Because I gave you life,
But you gave me a reason to live.

Flatland

It's wintertime in the Midwest.
A different vision here than all the rest.
For here the land is flat, and dull year round.
That is of course,
Until snow begins to fall onto the ground.
When the snow starts to stick,
There is no where you would rather pick
To spend the season.

I like the flatland in the wintertime.
I like the snow and coziness.
I love the people in all their loveliness.

Warm cup of cocoa, and peppermint candy.
A small glass of the region's best whiskey.
Sat around a fire with the curtains open.
The snow falls quietly against the window pane.

Once you experience a winter like this,
No other winter will ever be the same.

When everyone returns to their coastal towns,
They will miss the Midwest,
And miss the snow on the flatland ground.

January Days

The white fox prowls the fresh snow,
Leaving prints in it's path,
As a nearby rabbit enjoys the rising sun.

The warmth of the light,
Casts a tint over the blanket.
The long night has passed,
But a chill in the air remains.

The snowman is still standing in the front yard.
The children built him in December,
They worked so very hard.
His days are numbered, and that's alright.
When springtime comes,
They will fill with delight
As the flowers grow in his place.

The father is shoveling snow,
Before he heads off to work.
As the hibernating groundhog's head
Begins to perk.

The animals are still sleeping,
All but a few.
For January is too cold
To be awake, with me and you.

For now,
While the days are still cold.
We should enjoy it while it lasts.
Before the days grow old.

Sit in wonder, look and be amazed.
Take it all in,
On these January days.

Lights

The time has come,
When the clouds begin to grow.
Sprinkles first, then it begins to rain down snow.
The children fill with joy as they put on their boots,
And their mittens.
They then hug their mothers,
And pat the heads of their kittens.
They burst through the door as they embrace the snow.
It's been almost a year now
Since they've seen this show.
Then comes the nightfall,
And it's time to go inside.
But first they look around, and they're in for a surprise.

The neighbors all along the street begin to
Turn on their lights.
Hours and hours of decorating,
Just for the children's delight.

Those hours did not go unnoticed,
For the children did see,
A display of lights that filled them with glee.

The Road Home

It's been a long time,
Since I sat with you.
I wanted to call,
I still do.

I want to drive that long road home,
As long as it brings me to you.

Homesick doesn't begin to describe
What I'm feeling inside.
This place in my heart,
Where my hometown resides.

I miss my family,
My childhood friends.
I miss the ocean,
The trees, and the rain.

I miss my first home, where my child
Took his first steps.
Said his first words,
And I heard his first laugh.

I miss my son being around my family.
Those that he loved.
I miss seeing the look on your face,
As he held your hand.

Being far away,
Hurts me just as much as it hurts you.
I want to come closer,
But it might take me a little bit.

Though I know when I do,
It might take me a while to travel
The road home to you.

For my Family back home.

I miss you,
And I love you more
Than words can describe.

Lightning Source UK Ltd.
Milton Keynes UK
UKHW051907110822
407178UK00003B/121/J